For Nané & Cal
to read to your grandchildren.

May God Bless you,

Kristin McCullough

KING TRAVIS:

The Most Perfect Boy in the World

By
Alexandra Allred

Illustrations by
Kerri Allred

Kristin McCullough mother of
"King Travis"

5710 Buffalo St
Midlothian, Tx 76065
972 351 7380

To Kristin McCullough,
the Queen of all Mothers,
who fought for her baby and taught him to be king!
We thank you!

Published by Allredbooks
Dallas, Texas
Copyright © 2011 by Alexandra Allred

Visit www.allredbooks.com

ISBN: 978-0-9838230-6-3

Printed in the United States of America

September 2011

When Travis was born, he was different from other children. At first, he had trouble breathing and doctors did not know what was wrong with him. He could not crawl like the others when he was a baby and it took him a little longer to learn how to speak but his parents loved him so much!

To them, he was the most perfect boy in the world.

3

In school, while his friends learned to spell and do math, Travis had a much harder time. He was very smart but sometimes it was hard for him to learn the way the other children could. Many times, Travis got frustrated.

Sometimes, his classmates would tease him and that would make Travis sad. They did not understand that Travis has autism or that autism is something Travis was born with that made his brain and his muscles grow differently from other kids his age.

Still every day and every night, Travis' mother and father would tell him, "You're the most perfect boy in the world!"

But it was hard to believe his parents and even his sisters when other kids were playing sports and going to birthday parties and laughing together but they did not invite Travis.

"I am the most perfect boy in the world," Travis would say but he did not always believe it himself.

Travis' mother would tell him, "But you make us so happy. You are so sweet and so special to us. You are the most perfect boy in the world to us."

"You are not any different than us," his family would tell him! And just to prove it … they never expected Travis to be anyone but Travis, "the most perfect boy in the world."

Many times, in fact, Travis helped his own family discover who THEY were. Travis taught everyone around him to enjoy life and to be the best that they could be.

HOWDY

Hello!

HEY!

Hi!

Hello!

Howdy!

Hi!

hey!

Hi

Hello!

Travis was very kind and gentle. He did not call people names or say mean things to anyone. Travis was honest. He liked to make friends and always said "Hello" to everyone with a smile.

Travis continued to grow and one day he went to high school. As his classmates grew, they began to understand what autism was a little bit more. As those children got older, they began to see the very things Travis' family did.

Travis was very kind and gentle. He did not call people names and always said "Hello" to everyone in the hallways of the high school.

Still, Travis knew that he was different and he sometimes wondered if he was the most perfect boy in the world.

Travis, the most Perfect Boy in the World!!!!!!

By: Travis

As much as Travis' mother and father loved Travis, they often worried what other people thought of their son. They wished that other people could see how kind and gentle Travis was.

Then, one day the school took a vote. Who would be their Homecoming King? Who would be the King of their school? It had to be someone everyone liked. It had to be someone who was kind and gentle and said "Hello" to everyone he met.

Travis was named King!

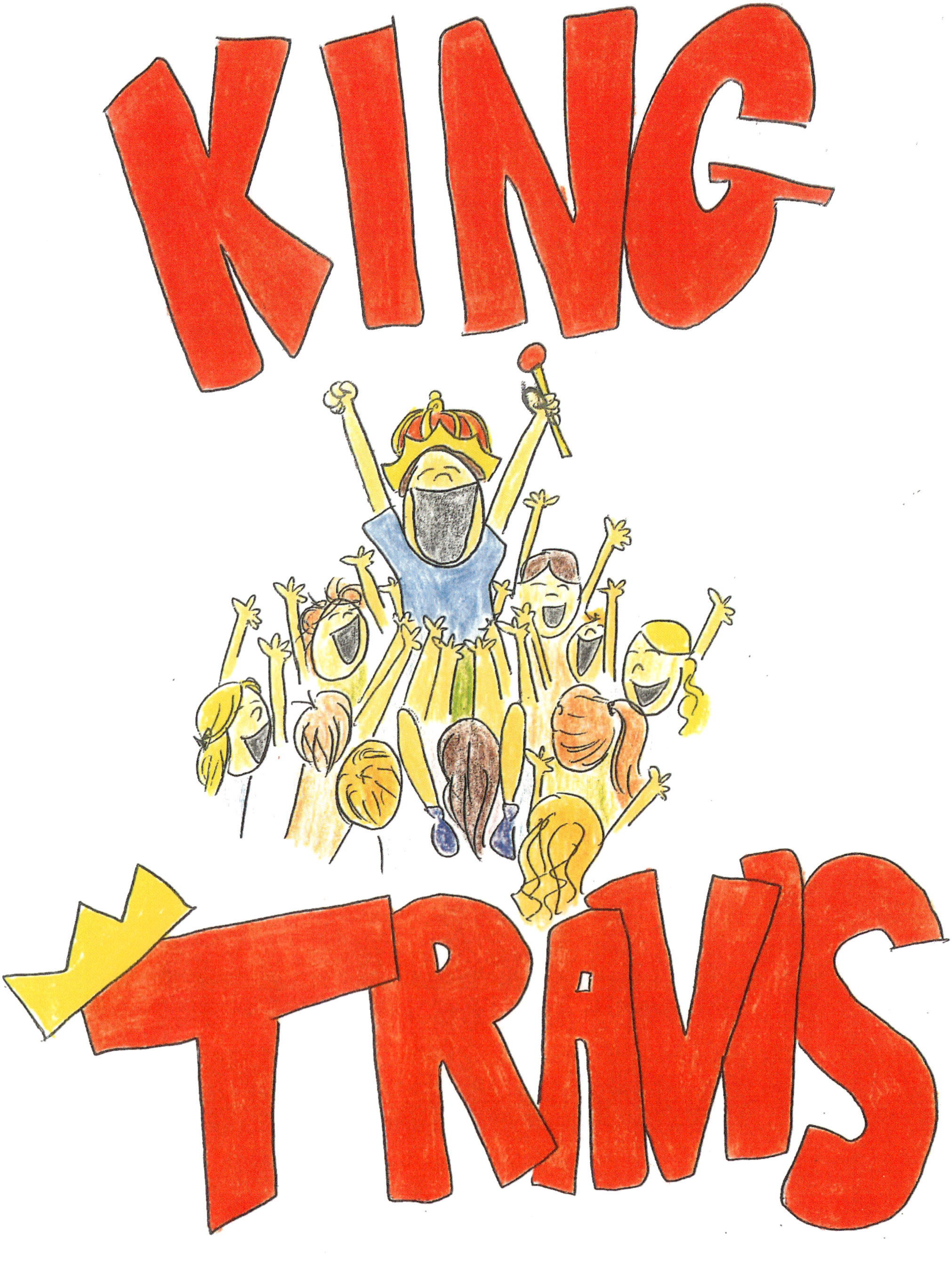
KING
TRAVIS

It did not matter that he could not play sports or march in the band or be the best speller. He was kind and gentle and he was KING!

And he knew, without a doubt, that he was the most perfect boy in the world.

THE END

About the Author, Illustrator, the Most Perfect Boy in the World, his Super Hero Family and a horse named Sammy ….

[details on how they met/pictures… Travis' true condition and a website to learn more about Travis]